PORTRAIT OF AN ARTIST

GEORGIA O'KEEFFE

ILLUSTRATED BY ALICE WIETZEL
WRITTEN BY LUCY BROWNRIDGE

WIDE EYED EDITIONS

Georgia O'Keeffe grew up on a wheat farm in place called Sun Prairie. Of all her six brothers and sisters, Georgia was the most thoughtful. She loved the big skies, vibrating orange sunshine, and beautiful flowers on the prairie.

When she looked at flowers or ears of corn, she would think very hard about the shapes of each tiny part and wondered how they could all possibly grow from the dry earth!

As soon as she was old enough, she went to art school in Chicago and New York City so she could learn how to make pictures of the beautiful things she saw in the world around her.

Living in the big city was wonderful. It was so busy and glamorous compared to the stillness of the farm. At art school she learnt how to paint very traditional things like dark shadowy bowls of fruit or bunches of flowers.

Although she loved New York, the pictures she made didn't fill her with the same wonder as the wide open landscapes she had loved at home.

One day, when Georgia was at art school, she got a letter from her mother who was very sick. Georgia had to move home and be with her.

When she went back, she started working in her old high school as an art teacher. She wanted to teach the children in a completely new way and not the stuffy way she had been taught.

Instead of making things look realistic, she encouraged her students to use bright colors and bold shapes and not to worry too much about whether you could tell what the picture was meant to be of.

Georgia loved teaching art, but still thought about the busy excitement of New York. She often wrote to her friend who still lived in the city and one day, she put a few of her sketches inside a letter to her.

Her friend saw that the drawings weren't ordinary but very special, so she passed them on to a man called Alfred Steiglitz. Alfred had been an important photographer and owned his own gallery.

Alfred was amazed by Georgia's drawings. He wrote to her to ask if she would do him the honor of showing her pictures in his gallery.

Georgia agreed and was nervous but excited. It was strange to be back in the big city and this time her art was on show in the hottest spot in town! She filled the show with charcoal drawings and watercolors and all sorts of glamorous people came to see what she had made.

Her success gave her a new confidence. She realised she could show people things they already knew but in a completely new way. This was her gift.

Georgia was proud of her show but not satisfied. She felt her charcoal pictures were bold but not colorful enough. And her watercolor pictures were colorful, but too watery!

She started to use oil paint because the colors were as bright and bold as the colors in nature. Oil paint could look as deep and velvety as the middle of jewel-like flowers.

And that is exactly what she started to paint. She wanted to make tiny flowers big, important and unmissable. They were so close-up, you could hardly tell what they were. No one had done this before.

As Georgia grew happier, she started to notice beauty in the city where she hadn't before. At first, the cold, harsh skyscrapers had made her feel small. Now their towering watch was comforting and made her feel powerful. The buildings looked as beautiful to her as mountains.

As she fell in love with New York, she also fell in love with Alfred. In no time at all, the pair were married and became towering giants of the New York art scene. The whole of New York waited to see what Georgia would paint next.

But Georgia didn't let the pressure get to her.
Georgia and Alfred were very happy. They traveled
together, and Georgia painted more and more. Alfred
even started taking photographs again. Georgia's
enthusiasm for life revived the artist inside him, too!

But Alfred was
much older than
Georgia and started
to become sick.

Alfred had to stay at home more and more and Georgia discovered new places by herself. She visited New Mexico, where the hot desert mountains gave her the same feeling of excitement as the big city skyscrapers had. They felt old and wise but also like something new and just for her.

The wide open space gave her time to think about new paintings and about the complicated feelings of sadness she had about Alfred being unwell.

Very soon, her beloved and inspiring Alfred passed away. While Georgia was terribly sad, she had so many ideas to put into her pictures. She started to paint more than ever and from now on, painting would become her entire life.

Now she was famous, everyone in the city
had an opinion on what her art meant, and
what she should do next.

But Georgia had no time for being bossed about by art
people in the city. New York was no longer the place for
her—nature was calling her back.

So she moved to New Mexico, where her heart leapt, just as it had the time she first painted flowers and then skyscrapers. Her new great love was the powerful shape of the mountains, the big sky, and the hot earth.

She lived in a house built from the red earth. It reminded her of the beautiful red mountains of the nearby Ghost Ranch, which always loomed large in her imagination. From the porch she even had a view onto what she called "her own private mountain." It was so far from people, she called it her "faraway nearby."

She felt that her new surroundings connected her to nature and the bare bones of life. She spent day after day, roaming the plains and finding strange objects that she couldn't wait to take home and paint.

One summer she traveled to show her paintings in Mexico and met another brilliant painter called Frida Kahlo. They became close friends and Georgia inspired Frida to follow her own path and not to listen to other people if they told her what she should paint. Frida listened very carefully and went on to become the most famous painter Mexico has ever seen.

Georgia was still busy. She flew all over the world opening shows and meeting glamorous people but after a while she wondered if that was what she wanted. As she looked out of the airplane window, she longed to be home and to paint the big skies.

As Georgia became older, and her eyesight
started to fade, she traveled less and less and
spent time where she had found real happiness.

Georgia had achieved more than she had ever imagined and was known the world over as the mother of American Modernism. She was pleased, but she didn't live to impress others.

All she lived for was the sky, the earth and to paint.
At last, she was peacefully alone in nature, with a brush in her hand.

WHAT'S IN THE MASTERPIECE?

UNTITLED (TEAPOT AND FLOWERS), 1903-5

Georgia painted this when she was just 18 years old. She used a watery paint which helped her make the yellow flower petals look really crinkly and lively against the sludgy background. She left a white gap on the teapot, which makes it look shiny.

EVENING STAR III, 1917

This picture is of a setting sun on a warm day with a blue sky and cool green field. Georgia manages to tell us all of this in just 6 simple strokes of paint.

EARLY ABSTRACTION, 1915

Pictures such as this one, that aren't of a specific thing you can recognise, are called "abstract." Sometimes abstract things remind us of objects we have seen before. Maybe you think it looks like the top of a violin. Or perhaps it reminds you of a flower about to unfurl and burst into bloom. What do you think inspired this picture?

SUNSET AND LITTLE CLOUDS NO. II, 1917

Georgia used the water in the watercolor paint to help the warm colors in the sunset bleed into each other.

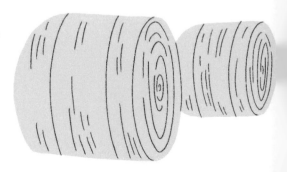

RITZ TOWER, NIGHT, 1928

The dark shadowy skyscraper with warm lights inside seems both spooky and inviting at the same time. Georgia said she didn't "paint New York as it is, rather as it felt."

JIMSON WEED, WHITE FLOWER NO. I, 1932

This little flower is part of a plant most people think of as a weed. Instead of ignoring this little weed, Georgia painted it big and put it in a gallery. Ever since, it has been admired and looked at as a great beauty rather than a little weed flower.

BLACK MESA LANDSCAPE, NEW MEXICO, 1930

If you think of a desert landscape you might imagine it all looking very yellow and hot, but there is almost no yellow in this picture. The pink mountain at the front looks hot, cracked and dry while the cold blue mountains behind seem shadowy and far away.

EAST RIVER FROM THE SHELTON HOTEL, 1928

Something Georgia loved about skyscrapers was that from the top of them, you could find a whole new viewpoint. Do you think it was warm or cold in New York when she painted this?

FROM THE FARAWAY, NEARBY, 1937

When Georgia painted this animal skull she found in the desert, she could have made it look frightening. Instead, she painted it in soft morning light which makes it seem calm and thoughtful.

SKY ABOVE CLOUDS IV, 1965

Georgia painted this after being inspired by clouds outside an aeroplane window. The puffy white clouds almost look like marshmallows floating on the sea. It feels like a scene from a dream. This is not a painting of exactly how the clouds looked, but of how Georgia remembered them.

IMAGES CREDITS

For Matteo – L.B.

Portrait of an Artist: Georgia O'Keeffe © 2020 Quarto Publishing plc.
Text © 2020 Quarto Publishing plc.
Illustrations © 2020 Alice Wietzel
Written by Lucy Brownridge

First published in 2020 by Wide Eyed Editions, an imprint of The Quarto Group.
400 First Avenue North, Suite 400, Minneapolis, MN 55401, USA.
T (612) 344-8100 **www.QuartoKnows.com**

A catalog record for this book is available from the British Library.
ISBN 978-0-7112-4879-3

The illustrations were created artwork created with digital media
Set in La Chic, Palomino Sans and Print Bold

Published by Georgia Amson-Bradshaw
Designed by Myrto Dimitrakoulia
Edited by Lucy Brownridge
Production by Dawn Cameron
Picture research by Jen Veall

Manufactured in Guangdong, China TT112019

1 3 5 7 9 8 6 4 2